Singing Back to the Sirens

Singing Back to the Sirens

Margaret DeRitter

For information contact:
Unsolicited Press
Portland, Oregon
www.unsolicitedpress.com
orders@unsolicitedpress.com
619-354-8005

Author Photo: Kaitlin LaMoine Martin
Cover Design: Kathryn Gerhardt
Editor: Nathaniel Burgess
ISBN: 978-1-950730-28-5

Contents

Epilogue

To Amy, for the years we shared

To Margy, for leading me back to joy and laughter and grand adventures

And to my mother, whose love was unending

I.

So Many Sang to Me

Their songs, though irresistibly sweet,
were no less sad than sweet . . .
— Walter Copland Perry on Homer's Sirens

THOSE FIRST SEVEN MONTHS

Cigar smoke curled through each day
like an umbilical cord. Strong brown

arms, a crisp white shirt drove me
in a basket on the back seat of a Pontiac

from home to home, yet nowhere really home,
and mother's milk from too many hands.

My father can list the names for her absence:
pleurisy, pneumonia, staph infection, D&C.

But what's a memory you don't remember—
a mythic catfish that can't be caught?

I could take it on faith or trust the evidence—
a dozen departed lovers stung by its barbs.

Sometimes my father would lay me on her chest.

WE COULD HAVE BURNED THE HOUSE DOWN

A pop can blasted with BB shots catches the sun
and I'm back at the Glen Rock dump with you
and our Daisy rifles, dungarees, army canteens.

I carried mine on a camouflage belt,
swigged from it like a thirsty soldier.
We used to walk the railroad tracks with
hobo sacks and Wonder Bread sandwiches.

People would mistake us for boys when we'd hide
our long, blond hair under baseball caps,
or sisters when we would let it down, but
you were nothing like a boy or sister to me.

When you passed me a note in third grade—
Can you come to my house after school?—
I felt that climbing-the-monkey-bars tingle
between my legs. Your eyes were those marbles
girls would hang on a chain—crackly and ravishing.

You let me in on the secrets of sex—
told me women covered themselves in rubber
down there, that homos took baths together.

We did that too—*Did that make us homos?*
I wondered as I blew Crazyfoam through
a washcloth and slathered it on your head.

I wanted to make Creepy Crawlers with you,
but my mother bought me Fun Flowers instead.
One day we forgot them in their little oven
when we went outside to build a fort.

You could have burned the house down,
my mother yelled. She must have smelled the smoke.

SUSIE AND ME AND THE LINE IN THE ROAD

Fall Saturdays at Green Pond we'd gather up chestnuts and stash them away for warrior necklaces. We were fierce then and loyal, fought any kids we didn't like—with words. One time we drew a line across the road and dared some Shadyside punks to cross it. A few years later it was Susie who crossed that line, started hanging out with those punks, smoking dope on the beach, outside the reach of streetlights. Sometimes when I'd walk my dog alone at night, I'd see her there in the shadows, laughing, cool as a saxophone riffing on a new tune.

WONDERLAND

My first memory of you isn't even a memory—
it's the two of us standing beneath a trellis
of roses in my front yard, holding hands and posing.
for my father's camera. A slide that would cement
that day into childhood history.

We played school and Colorforms
on my front porch, fought over Monopoly money,
faked a wedding ceremony on your front steps,
marched home in solidarity when a bully girl
tipped my baby carriage over in the street.

We dressed up each year for the masquerade party
and won awards for your cousin's creativity—
the Pepsi Generation one year, Alice in Wonderland
and the Queen of Hearts the next, your younger
brothers the Mad Hatter and March Hare.

The firemen's fair signaled the end of summer.
We tossed nickels onto glass dishes and slid
across Scrambler seats together, pledged
to keep in touch all winter. And did, even
spending weekends overnight.

At twelve and thirteen we were too young for Woodstock
and envied our big brothers. 'Suite: Judy Blue Eyes'
was our anthem the next summer. We played that
record raw on your front porch as your brothers'
electric guitars screamed in the background.

We thought we were cool when we'd hang out
evenings at the Community House, punching
numbers into the jukebox for 'Summer in the City'
and 'San Francisco,' the flower song. Was I already
falling in love with girls? Maybe you saw it.

Or maybe you just moved on.
One morning I showed up at your back door,
the way I had for years, and your mother
said you'd already left. I didn't get it—
till I saw you at the beach with other friends.

I locked my bedroom door and let James Taylor
sing my silver tears to sleep. The month before,
after my eighth grade graduation, we'd eaten sundaes
with my family at the Barn. We were going to travel
the country in a VW bug when I turned twenty-one.

In time I found new friends to get me through,
built a fresh array of Jersey snapshots—
days in the ocean at Island Beach, nights
on the coasters at Seaside Heights, music
on the grass off the Garden State Parkway.

This summer when James Taylor opened a Michigan
concert with 'Carolina in My Mind,' I was carried back
to Jersey. A friend looked over and saw me cry.
I could feel the sunshine of those Green Pond
summers, hear the highway's call again.

A few months later I sat in your mother's house
trading stories and hugs with you and your brothers.
The years peeled away but not the surreal. I was Alice
down a rabbit hole. You kept mentioning friends you met
after me. As if I'd remember. As if I could ever forget.

DRIVING TO THE JERSEY SHORE

Friday nights when the factory whistle blew,
you'd pop some Springsteen into your tape deck
and we'd head out on the interstate, from Fairfield
to Pine Brook, West Caldwell to East Orange,
and onto the Garden State Parkway.

That's when you'd floor it for the Jersey Shore
and the glorious names would accelerate—
Cheesequake, Red Bank, Asbury Park,
Sea Girt, Manasquan, Neptune City,
Barnegat, Brigantine, Margate.

Once, we pulled off early, at Long Beach Island,
to watch the sun climb over the ocean.
It started off a smidge of lava,
then exploded into a fireball,
burning as hot as Bruce's 'Badlands.'

We never made it to Avalon, Wildwood, Cape May,
but I loved the sounds of those Jersey towns
almost as much as the sea-salt air,
the warm night wind, the darkness
edging the dashboard lights.

Yes, I know, you had a lifeguard
you longed to see in Atlantic City,
but I had you inside that car
for those three hours
that whole sweet summer.

LEAVING CALVIN FOR *LA CAGE*

I find the letter in my college newspaper—
there's a gay support group in town—
Oh, my God, is this my chance to leave the fold?

I want to go. I'm terrified.
There might be flying monkeys.

One Sunday night a year I was allowed to skip church
with my brother to watch *The Wizard of Oz.*
Those creatures sent me running to my room
every time they showed up on the screen.

I meet the letter writer for a talk.
He's blond and blue-eyed just like me,
like so many Dutch kids from Calvin College.
Shallow, I know, but he makes me feel safe.
Like Uncle Henry and the farmhands.

He invites me to a Dignity meeting.
We're going to a movie, he says.

It's not *The Wizard of Oz,* it's *La Cage,*
but it feels like a tornado's coming.

Our group fills the Bijou.
Father Wayne is a cut-up,
Father Dan has a boyfriend,
Sister Candy a girlfriend.

Holy shit, Scarecrow! Who are these people
who've been hiding under the flowers
just waiting to come out and sing?

Can I join their merry guild?
Would Kansas ever take me back?

FIRST GAY BAR

I can picture that black Carousel door even now,
nearly forty years later, my hand hesitating
as I reached for the silver handle, a friend nudging
my back, my tennis shoe crossing the threshold.

Was I Columbus setting foot in the New World
or Eve reaching for the forbidden fruit?
Was this sin or salvation? Or both?
My heart and history were fighting it out.

But Donna Summer was calling from inside,
and I needed some hot stuff that summer.
As my new friends clapped and cheered,
I followed her onto the dance floor.

FIRST GIRLFRIEND: VALENTINE'S DAY, 1981

My friend and I wore matching wigs, reverse outfits—
red overalls, white shirt; white overalls, red shirt.
We were Raggedy Anne and Andy. Went to a gay bar
like that. Can't you feel the sex appeal?

And yet I met my first girlfriend that night—
after I lost the wig. She was a gym teacher.
I know, such a cliché, but she was wiry, muscled,
tan, loved to play tennis and sunbathe naked
in the dunes. And the teacher thing, oh yeah.

She offered me a ride home via her place.
The next day: a film to watch for work,
a co-worker sitting beside me in the dark
and me vibrating with all I couldn't say.

I STILL SMELL THE SMOKE

Your girlfriend's in Norway
and the shower is running
and we're both twenty-four
and you're pulling my red dress
over my head and the soft
of your breasts is pressing
my back and the smoke
on your skin is the essence
of sex and we're sliding like seals
and swallowing water
with each urgent kiss.

I could say that we burst
like hydrangeas in May
but I wouldn't call us flowers.
We were slathered in sweat
and salt and slippery desires.
We had urges so strong
they could melt away cities,
blow away fjords, explode
her existence.

It's true—I wanted her gone.
Not dead, just vanished,
but you banished me instead.
And now as you sit beside me

and pull out your phone
to show me your son—her son—
I smile politely, say the right words,
but I still smell the smoke
on your skin, still taste the sweat,
still feel the burn of that summer.

OH YEAH, YOU LIKE BOYS

You seem a little nervous when I pick you up
and you're dressed real sweet as if this
were a date, but, oh yeah, you like boys.

You ask me if I'd like a Coke and sit beside me
on the couch and we talk so long that going out's
an afterthought, but, oh yeah, you like boys.

You show me naked women you've drawn in sexy poses,
even the one above your bed, but there's a damn snake
lurking underneath her legs. Something to do with boys?

We go to dinner and stay so late we miss the first site
on the gallery slate, but I don't mind and you don't seem to
and I could stay forever with you. Something to do with girls.

When we get to the art, you stand so close I could trace
your smile, your eyes, your nose, and I feel the heat
of your breath on my skin and almost forget again—
Oh yeah, you like boys.

When we're driving home, you suggest dessert and soon
we're talking ice cream floats and gooey sundaes
and the ones we order are big and chocolatey and slide down
smoothly and we barely notice the boy who says it's time to
          leave.

Then you tell me you'd love to see my house sometime
so I take you home and we sit on my sofa oh so close
that I feel your thigh so soft and you don't move away
as I show you scenes of mountains and beaches where I wish
you'd been. And there aren't any boys in these pictures.

You say you like the color of my hair and tell me I look great
        in pink
before we head to my bedroom, but this is just the home tour
        visit,
not the real one—is it?—though you do like my sleigh bed
and I'd love to take you for a ride. Can't we leave the boys
        behind?

SINGING BACK TO THE 'STRAIGHT' GIRL

Here's a poem for all the girls who fall for other girls who
  never
look their way when it's time for love, who keep on chasing
  them
anyway, who never shun the siren girl who says she's straight
but sings her crooked songs to all the passing lesbians.

That girl will lick the ice cream off your spoon, then feign
  surprise
when she sees you swoon. She'll hum real sweet and sit real
  close
but would never consider a full-throated kiss. Give in just
  once,
she knows, and she might not snag a sailor boy's ship.

So here's what to do if she's singing to you:
Sing louder than her. Sing stronger. Sing higher. Sing longer.
Drown her out. Blast her out. Blow her away with your sexiest
  sax.

Or hum really low like a cigarette's glow. Purr in her ear
like a Siamese cat. Sidle up with your violin and sing
your own sweet songs to lure her in.

BLUE

I remember blue ice cubes sliding down my belly
toward my leather belt, an aqua water slide
and you in the blue of a small-town pool,

your cornflower eyes in the back seat of a Buick
the night I met you, the months I waited
for your royal-blue dress to slide to the floor.

I traced the blue-green veins at your elbow
as we lay beneath your cobalt quilt
in a moon-draped room.

On a bluff above the Pere Marquette
we pitched a slate-blue tent, then soothed
our sunburned skin in the cool of the river.

The azure skies of Arizona kicked up black
thunderclouds across the Grand Canyon
as we ran for refuge from the rain.

Under the mocking blue of a summer sky
we biked our grudges past blackberry fields,
looming spruces, murky ponds.

Blue was not the only plate I'd eat from.
Not the color I wanted for a couch.
Not what I saw when you closed your door.

But you still wore blue when you
stopped by to pick up your boots,
my black dog glad to see you.

PADDLING THE WILDERNESS

We found Tom Thomson in a Toronto museum,
his paintings of Canada's landscapes
as colorful as a Caribana parade.

A waiter told us about Algonquin,
and those two girls on the dock with dirty
bandannas from a week's worth of wild
made us long for our own adventure.

The next summer we paddled Canoe Lake
to Little Joe to Burnt Island and stopped to camp
when black flies made meals of our necks.

At night the moon drew a path to us,
and loons cried out across the water.
We made tea and double-boiler chocolate
that we scooped with graham crackers.

We wanted to mate for life
but, like Michigan winters, your moods
turned gray and I grew stormy.

In Chicago you locked me out of our hotel room.
In Kalamazoo I threw a telephone at the floor.
Yet our love kept calling across the waves,
diving and surfacing year after year.

GONE

She's in love with the boy
and even if they have to run away
she's gonna marry that boy someday.
—*Trisha Yearwood*

I change the word to *girl*
and sing you that country song—
you at the kitchen sink,
me heading out for work.

You wipe soap on your apron,
hold my face in your hands
to say goodbye.

But when I get home, no smells
come floating from the oven,
no music from the stereo.

It takes a moment to notice
the half-empty coat rack,
a moment longer to take it in.

And then I see your green goose
gone above the kitchen door,
one apron on the hallway hook,
one bookshelf in the living room.

I find your note in the dining room,
then crawl upstairs to bed.

Across the hall, where you hung
your paintings, the walls are a picked
sunburn, patchy and raw.

The scratches on the wooden floor
the only sign of your tall oak dresser.

FLOATING THROUGH HADES ON A PIN CUSHION

The cottage at Green Pond has turned
into gingerbread. It's crawling with ants.

Donald Trump has taken an interest
in the last pink motel in Palm Beach.

The woman I loved is laughing
in the windows of every party I walk past.

A slug falls from my nightgown,
a silvery line runs down my thigh.

Black flies are migrating to Michigan
in V-formations.

Something's shaking under the house,
the plaster's cracking, my teeth are loose.

An arm grows from my chest.
It flops like a fish at the light switch.

SHOOTING ANGELS: MENDON, MICHIGAN

Sunday afternoon and I've found the old stone church.
Across the road, centuries of granite and limestone,
name upon name eroded by time and rain.

She used to shoot angels here—her Mendon series.
Today I shoot angels and headstones and Jesus,
then drive to the old brick schoolhouse, where ivy claws
and climbs the mortar she restored with a lover's care.

She thought a one-room home and small-town life
would make her muse return. Instead they made her long
for Kalamazoo, where she found me—substitute muse,
dependable shelter, immovable star.

On Sundays we would drive down Silver Street to roam
the graves and sit outside the schoolhouse in her car.
She needed to know her abandoned treasure
was still well tended.

On those days we'd walk the St. Joe River, watch birds fly off
toward Centreville. She'd point to David and Sarah's house.
She loved their studio, their gardens, their marriage—
the idea of it all.

Nesting was her specialty, her safety net,
her terror. She flew back from California once.
We sat in a car outside my house.

THE ROMANCE OF BACKLIT GRASSES

Evening sun lights up native grasses
as I drive down a Michigan highway
that splits the heart of my chosen state.

Once, my love told me she could hardly bear
the hills of California, their sun-bleached
grass too close a match to my blond hair.

I spent hours walking alone in Jersey meadows
when I was a girl dreaming of other girls.
Those Glen Rock grasses had California colors.

The grasses here are summer green.
They remind me of no one's hair, and yet
I feel the bones of my chest breaking open

and something like love or nostalgia
rushing out to nestle in those grasses,
those beautiful backlit grasses.

HOW CALVINISM CAME BETWEEN US

Yes, I know, my mother loved me beyond measure,
never even shunned my women lovers
for fear of losing me.

Margaret's coming home with her friend,
she told people in 1983.

Margaret bought a house with her friend,
she told people twenty-three years later.

But she couldn't—wouldn't—say *girlfriend.*
Didn't ask much about those women either.

I never got to hear: *How did you meet?*
What do you like about her?
Do you think you'll get married?

Those were the questions she saved for
my nephew, who dated the appropriate sex.

One time I traveled all the way to Florida
to cry with her when a girlfriend left me.

I just want you to be happy, my mother said.
It was the best thing I ever heard.

Decades later, finally happy, I told her
of my new love. She barely smiled.

She used to say she'd walk through fire for me.
She must not have foreseen my fire for women.

She'd been raised on Leviticus, the letters
of Paul, her church's statement on gays.
What more did I expect?

I knew the answer the night she died,
when anger took me by surprise:
A lot more. A whole lot more.

BREAKFAST AT SIMPLY CELIA'S, WHERE NOTHING IS SIMPLE

The woman I loved in college has a lesbian daughter—
she drops this news as if it were the weather.

We don't talk about the day she thought I might kiss her
but didn't as we sat on the dunes beside Lake Michigan.

She wrote about that once, said she wasn't sure
whether she felt relieved or disappointed.

One time in college we stayed up half the night
before I could get the words out: *I think I'm gay.*

When I finally did, she answered, *Oh, I knew that,*
but I thought it was important for you to say it first.

Now I want her to say it first—
not that she's gay, but that she remembers

that day at the beach, the story she sent me,
the feelings she had that weren't always simple.

I want her to tell me she told her daughter our story,
but instead she tells me she's always loved men.

Sometimes lately I don't even like her,
but today, as we leave, I love how she ties her coat.

TWO DAYS AFTER A CANCELED
KNEE REPLACEMENT

I slice an S through paper-white snow
on my favorite slope, my knees growing bolder
with every turn, every run.

Ah, the graceful weightlessness,
the thrilling speed as I tease the edges
of fear and control.

Got hooked on this sport at seven years old.
At sixty, I'm in love with it still—
the minty smell of winter air, sun on snow,

silent trees, squeaky chairs where I hang
like a spider and remember the days
when Sabich skied the World Cup circuit.

I saw him once at a Catskills resort,
Wide World of Sports filming his turns
as he flew through the flags.

Another weekend at Hunter Mountain
our English teacher slid off a slope
as we waited at the school bus.

I can't remember her name—no, wait,
it was Stiles, Mrs. Emily Stiles, and I yearned
to be the one who would save her.

My friends didn't know that about me.
I made fun of her instead, the way I pretended
to hate my gym teacher.

God, how did I end up here with this poem?
Is it always about longing?
Can I never let it go?

Maybe the truth is I don't want to.
After all, look where it got me today—
out of my easy chair, over my fear

of aging and injury, back to my first love,
wind grazing my face, decades falling away
as I carve the softening snow.

AT THE TOP OF SLEEPING BEAR DUNES

A giant sign warns visitors to think twice
about descending. It could cost a rescue fee
or, for the lucky ones, a two-hour climb.
I did it once, at twenty-five, with my first gay
friend. We strolled the shoreline at the bottom
looking for shells—and an easier ascent—
then climbed back the way we came.
I lost him later to San Francisco.

At thirty-five I lay in the dunes with a lover
till a hang glider surprised us overhead.
I scurried back into my purple suit
and shorts the color of cantaloupe.
She took my photo by a bleached-out tree.
I lost her to California too and early
Alzheimer's. Last time we talked
she was dreaming of Mexico.

At forty-five I brought my parents here,
held my father's arm to help him
up the boardwalk to a bench.
My brother and I were still
talking then. He took my father's
other arm. My girlfriend stayed

at the cottage, said her head hurt.
We lasted a few more months.

Ten years later my wife and I stood
on the new wooden overlook,
its pillars sunk deep in the dune,
my knees, though, wobbly with fear.
I thought we'd keep coming back
year after year, watch our faces
grow old in photos, sink our own
supports deep in this sand.

Today I'm sixty. It's Mother's Day
and I'm an orphan, and my new lover
holds my arm to help me reach
the wooden bench. One knee has a torn
meniscus, the other arthritic spurs.
But that stand of trees at the crest
of the dune looks as lovely as ever,
as solid as anything can be.

II.

Singing Back to Her

I have dreamed in the grotto
where the siren swims . . .
— Gérard de Nerval

THE ALCHEMISTS HAD NOTHING
ON YOU

Was it your freckled skin that did me in
or the smell of cloves upon your neck?
Was it that smile that took up half your face
or the cheekbones that rose and curved
beside your perfect nose? Maybe it was your
narrow shoulders or gently jutting collarbones,
your lively brows or that space beneath your throat.
Maybe it was the way you held my packages
so I could find my keys or how you pressed your palm
beneath my belt and said, *There, that's the place I want to be.*
Maybe it was all those things that did their alchemy
on me. I followed your ambulance to that hellhole
in Pertuis, even emptied your bedpan there. Oh, God—
I would have followed your ass anywhere.

WATOGA STATE PARK

I handled the mountain driving.
You held your breath. We could see the treetops
at the edge of the road. It was nighttime
before we arrived at the old wooden cabin
built by the Civil Conservation Corps,
its chestnut walls salvaged from local mills.
Logs were stacked outside. You rearranged
living room chairs so we could watch the fire.

Next day we hiked to Bailey's Lookout.
Your toes froze together inside your new boots.
Raynaud's syndrome, you said. I took them out
and warmed them with my breath.
That evening I baked pork chops for you
like my mother's, smothered in rice, onions,
tomato soup. It was the first time you loved pork.
I should have kept cooking it for you.

The second morning we awoke to an early spring,
hiked a streamside trail and sat beside it in our shirts.
The hills were swathed in mountain laurel. It was blooming
in my imagination. The whole world was a garden.
Even the skunk that sprayed outside our bedroom window
made us laugh. The night was so dark I felt like Anne Frank.
No, I mean Helen Keller, I said. *One of those girls.*
The mix-up sent us into hysterics at four in the morning.

Day three we arose to a blanket of snow.
You tried my cross-country skis on the hill
near the cabin. We laughed when you fell,

your bones still strong, the snow a cushion.
Even the sudden change of weather seemed
enchanting. Yes, we were afraid of the drive out,
so we stayed and hiked till the snow disappeared.
It was gone before noon.

NOVICES AT SACRÉ-COEUR

Basilica of the Sacred Heart—built by war's exhausted ones
as penance for sin, place of unending prayers for peace—
called to us with its gleaming domes, white as wedding doves
or newly laundered sheets.

Novices at conflict, intent on romance, we walked the aisles
through incense and dust motes as a choir's voices rose
to the roof's mosaic, wrapping us in a wreath of song,
cocoon of harmony.

It was such delicate shelter, such deceptive joy,
but how could we have known it that sunny Paris day?
Above us, Jesus stretched his tiled arms in blessing,
his golden heart aglow.

SUMMER VACATION: MASON COUNTY, MICHIGAN

Eighty-nine steps from the cement-block cottage
and, halfway down, a deck for coffee and hummingbird
      feeders.
Our Labrador had freedom to roam, to sniff out bones
in the nearby grove and gnaw them on the sand.

At night he'd lie with us beside the fire, our faces glowing
through an open shutter. We were unguarded then,
didn't mind squeezing hip-to-hip in the skinny kitchen
or climbing over each other's legs into the tall oak bed.

In the daytime we'd walk Nicky down a dusty road
into the woods and out to a meadow filled with yellow
towers of mullein and noonday sunshine.
All I remember sometimes is the sunshine.

In Scottville you sat on a curb to watch the clowns
play saxophones and clarinets. I took photographs
of their orange hair and bright plaid pants,
of tourists dressed in clown band shirts.

You wore a sleeveless shirt that day,
leaned your arms against the sidewalk,
flexed your muscles to perfection.
I clicked my shutter, then leaned on you.

We were old enough to remember sideshows:
midgets, giants, sword swallowers.

The calliope brought it all back again
as if we were young and knew each other then.

WEDDING CATHEDRAL

Something about the light beneath those trees
transformed Dave's lawn to a green cathedral.
The first time I entered, alone, the world grew still
and dust motes floated in the sun.

Today the tents are up and music's moving
on the air. A hundred chairs await their guests.
You're putting on your wedding dress
bouqueted in pinks and blues and yellows.

When I see a flower in your hair,
I hear that San Francisco song I used to play
when I was young and dreamed of kissing girls
with flowers in their hair.

My cousin starts the processional song.
Your sister turns and smiles at us.
You lift your shoulders in a happy shrug.
I feel the trees exhaling.

AVALANCHE

It started with the pooping problems,
our dog squatting longer and longer,
tumor on the X-ray, no way to operate.

Then my mother's legs red and swollen,
sign of heart failure, her kidneys
too tired to handle the meds.

Near the end, dog enemas
in the back yard, keeping Nicky alive
through my mother's funeral—

then lifting him onto the cold steel,
feeling him collapse into my chest,
eighty pounds of avalanche.

A week's escape to West Virginia,
a phone call upon our return,
a special meeting at work—

I was afraid someone had died,
but, no, my job was gone,
twenty-two years and done.

DATELINE: KALAMAZOO

December 2011

For eighty-six years the Gazette stood granite-solid
at Burdick and Lovell. Now it's moving to a storefront
on the mall. Seventy journalists are down to nine,
though some may be rehired by a renamed,
revamped company that gives out news for free.

A new press pumped out its first edition
just eight years ago, rollers whirring,
paper spinning, folders folding, clips grabbing
each section, winders whipping pages
onto giant spools that would later unwind
them into News and Sports before they flew
out the door to pickups, vans, and beat-up old cars.

We were an army then—carriers, accountants,
sales crew, artists, designers, editors, reporters,
the lady on the phone with a real live voice.
We called the new section *Today,* with no clue
about tomorrow. We even threw a party
with tours and punch and praises for the pretty
clock tower high above the press.

One day we surrounded our three-story beast
by the hundreds, climbing its metal stairs
like kids up a slide, lining its skinny catwalks,
jostling for spots amid paper and ink.
We were Newspaper of the Year.

The photo looked like a celebration,
but layoffs crouched in the corner.

Consolidation with Grand Rapids had already
begun: accounting first, then ad creation,
classifieds, copy editing, printing. The paper rolls off
another press now, at midnight, sixty miles away,
the promise of a high-speed German machine
never to be realized in this city of The Promise.
Its hulking silhouette lies still behind glass,
a decommissioned soldier.

THANKSGIVING EXPLOSION

I'd like to blame my brothers.
They refused to attend our wedding.

Religious reasons, they said.
What a graceless God, I thought.

When one brother stopped talking to me,
I begged you to call the other to intervene.

Why don't YOU call him? you asked.
I can't, I said. *I want to drive into a tree.*

You promised to call him but never did.
At Thanksgiving your family filled our house.

I wanted to hear my brother's jokes,
eat my grandmother's cranberry salad,

play a board game after dinner.
Could you see if your family would play?

Why don't YOU ask them? you said,
and with that, my head exploded—

every grievance spattered on the kitchen walls,
the stove, the floor, the cupboards.

Do you really want to do this now? you asked.
Well, yes, yes, I wanted to do it now.

And I did it. Loud. And long. And there was no cleaning it up. And no one else to blame.

THAT DAY IN JANUARY

Come sit down, you said.
And the wave rose up.
I thought someone had died.

I have to leave,
you said, and seawater
crashed against my chest.

UNCOUPLING

You come through the *front* door now,
reach down to hug the dog,
look up at me with a shrug.
What else is there to do?

I hold my arms at my sides like some shy
audience member called on stage
by Letterman. But their nerves vibrate
as if two phantom limbs are reaching out.

They think you're still my wife,
can feel your charge,
the alternating current—
there and not there.

I HAD A GRANDDAUGHTER FOR
SEVEN MONTHS

Held her at five days,
fed her once at Thanksgiving,
went wild on clothes for her
at Christmas, and a blue dog.

I loved to watch her swim
in the bathtub, arms flailing,
legs kicking like a frog
who'd just sprouted limbs.

You gave me a brag book
filled with photos of our girl,
waited till January to announce
your departure.

There was no drama in December,
no conflict, just jigsaw puzzles,
a warm oven and endless
snowstorms.

We shoveled together,
raked the roof of our house
to prevent ice dams
or sudden collapse.

No one from your family
has called. The last time I saw
the baby on FaceTime
she looked ready to crawl.

I WANT TO MARRY MY INSURANCE GUY

He kayaks and speaks gently
and knows about broken houses.

He came by quickly
to inspect the ice damage.

His belly peeked out when
he reached for the ceiling,

his brown sweater just like
the one I wear from Macy's.

He showed me how his
measuring device worked,

beaming a laser from wall
to bathroom wall.

When the mirror made it fail,
he said, *You can't always trust*

these things. You have to
pay attention.

We sat at my kitchen table
so he could write an estimate.

He loved the sunlight,
the blue walls, couldn't stop

talking about boats
and rivers and wilderness.

I wanted him to stay
forever.

Before he left, he wrote
a check, without a fight,

said he hopes to see me
sometime on the water.

CARRYING HOME TO HOGSETT LAKE

The first turtle of spring
floats at the water's edge, dead,
upended, covered in sludge.
Did the harsh winter kill it
or years of toxic waste?
A ferocious bird?

Beneath the surface, webbed feet
flap to escape my shadow.
Other turtles scramble from shore
or jump from logs, then pop
their heads above the surface,
surrounding me with wary stares.

Like your looks from the kitchen
or the yellow chair. For seven years
we made a home together, made meals,
beds, love. But the snow was relentless
that winter, the wind too strong.
You pulled your tender skin inside
and left before spring.

Now my home is a kayak on Hogsett Lake,
loud with conversation of kingfishers,
blackbirds, crows.

I lift the dead turtle with my paddle—
surprised by its heft—then flip it
to inspect its neck, its snout, its shell,

find nine tiny spikes at the front
and wonder—useless vestige
or necessary protection?

Later I find it's the spiny softshell
kind. They hide in mud and sand,
bite hard, but only if provoked.

Unlike most other turtles,
they have no bony armor
to protect their shell.

CLOSING OUR ACCOUNT

I cried on the cashier's check
when we closed our account

the paper all wet
and see-through

I had no words left,
you offered none

when my face crumpled,
you reached for my hand

your hand so warm, so soothing,
so ready to withdraw

KINDS OF QUIET

I. Algonquin Park

Morning mist on Hailstorm Creek
Raindrops on a sheltered cove
Cooling embers in a campsite fire
Full moon mirrored on Little Joe Lake
No motors buzzing, no phones ringing

II. The 402

Blue Water Bridge arching the St. Clair River
Lake Huron spread to the edge of the Earth
Sailboats small as bathtub ships racing for the horizon
Sixth day with a traveling companion who isn't you
Arlo Guthrie singing 'A Hobo's Lullaby'

III. Home

Hauling gear into an empty house
No phones ringing, no messages blinking
Spreading the rain fly to dry in the yard
Watering all the plants that have wilted
Pouring coffee back into its jar

DREAM SEQUENCE: THE ROOF LEAKED WHEN YOU MOVED BACK IN

and moss spread across it like algae choking a summer pond. All the knives lay neatly in the drawer, but we heard them talking among themselves. We were afraid to speak, tried to guard the future with our silence. Our air sacs had grown stiff with age. The walls breathed for us. A bluebird, let in by a torn screen, sat at the kitchen sink, sipping from the faucet. It could fly out the same way it flew in.

ALL OF WRIGHT'S HOUSES LEAK

And, Lord knows, they never let in
enough light, but Frank grew up building

with Froebel blocks and learning to think
he was special. After all, his mother said it.

He married Kitty in 1889 and built
their home on an Oak Park prairie,

filled it with angles and artwork
and children and playrooms, but when

his daughters dared to hang up curtains,
he tore them down—they covered his lines.

And when the neighbor's Victorian came too close,
he plastered his windows to hide it from sight.

He was a master of design but
never cared much for the people inside.

Twenty years after the wedding
he rented the house to strangers,

put his family in his work space
next door and took a replacement wife.

But he failed to win a divorce—
Kitty drew her own line.

LET ME DRAPE THEM IN DIAMONDS

Our friend tells me you have *triple negative cancer.*
I try to breathe. I hear *triple X,* as in extreme,
pornographic, imagine a scalpel slicing your breasts.

Hormones can't stop it or slow it down, our friend says.
It takes stronger treatments.

At the card table, they perched inside your sweater.
At the kitchen sink I cupped them from behind.
In your penguin pajamas the flannel disguised them.

*Only chemo can kill this kind of cancer, but
the odds aren't good if the cells have spread.*

I remember the sun taunting me the day you left,
scattering diamonds on the snow. I want to make
a necklace now to drape across your chest.

*She wasn't planning to tell you, but I gave her a choice:
'You do it or I will. Margaret deserves to know.'*

I hurl the diamonds at the wall,
then slowly pick them up again.

IF *FRIEND* HAD AS MANY VARIATIONS AS ARCTIC SNOW

I'd have a word for the friend who shows up on my Facebook
        list
but never on party invitations, who clicks on all the animal
        videos
I post and tells me *Happy Birthday* online but never in
        person.
That word would sound nothing like *friend.*

I'd need an ambiguous word for the man I talk to every
        Sunday after church
who translates Dutch when I need it and knows where I go on
        vacations
and whether my knee is aching but who never asked about my
        wife.
After all, she didn't go to church and wasn't my husband.

The women in my writing group would come up with their
        own word,
maybe something with a hint of muse or cattle prod or the
        slow bloom
of a Madagascar palm. We started out sharing only poems,
        but now we play
extreme croquet and discuss replacement parts for aging limbs.

There's a good word already for the friend who saw me
        through every
breakup known to woman, fed me spaghetti and challah and
        sarcasm

before she moved to Chicago, and still invites me to her kids'
        graduations,
bat mitzvahs and birthday parties—she's a mensch.

I'd add a sassy sound for the man who took me to my first gay
        film, first gay bar,
spun me around that Carousel floor as it rained down men
        and lesbians,
watched me head home with my first woman lover, made up a
        nickname only
he ever called me, and flew to my wedding more than thirty
        years later.

And I haven't even gotten to the friend whose memories
        stretch back
with mine to 'American Pie' on a school bus ride. We sang it
        straight through
to the very last line, and I can imagine us singing that song till
        the day we die.
There's gotta be a word for someone I've loved such a long,
        long time.

After my wife left me, another friend lent me her own family,
        her brother's tortillas,
her sisters' casino trips, sat with me as my wife's cronies
        yukked it up over
Dunkin Donuts and styrofoam coffees the day they hauled her
        stuff
from our house. *Have some compassion,* she scolded, *and
        settle the fuck down.*

I could have loved her the whole damn way to Mexico just for
    that,
but she also called every morning for months. *Hey, are you*
    still alive?
Get your ass out of bed, you lazy oaf. She deserves a word all
    her own—
part *sister,* part *smart ass,* part *saint.*

WHEN GRIEF TURNS TWO

Think how the smell of a sulfurous egg
makes it hard to consider anything else.
It's not like that. Not always.

It's not a skunk or a jackhammer
or a garbage truck stuck in reverse.
It's not the neighbor's lawn mower.

It's the buzz of a fluorescent bulb—
once you notice, it won't let go.

AFTER THE CONFEDERATE FLAG CAME DOWN

I came upon a wedding guest list tucked inside a legal pad. I needed the pad for a workshop: 'Racial Issues in the LGBT Community.' But the list? What was I hanging on to—the way you once loved me? I know it wasn't perfect, but what is? Hell, if love required perfection, there'd be no love at all. I was in a mood before I ever walked into that workshop. Then we had to name our preferred pronouns. I wanted to say *this* and *that*. I know trans people suffer, but do we really need to make an 80-year-old straight guy with a beard say *he, him, his?* By the time someone said *hetero-normative*, I was sick of words. It helped when Lester told us he was there because his gay son died in a car accident. Plain English. Real grief. The next day a newspaper photo caught my eye: black cop guiding sun-baked supremacist up South Carolina stairs toward air-conditioning. The cop looked sure on his feet, the white guy ready to topple onto his swastika. It was the day the Confederate flag came down at the state house. A reporter asked the cop why he thought the photo went wild on the internet. *Love,* he said. *I think that's the greatest thing in the world—love.* Yes, *that,* I thought, breaking down at last—for you and me, for Lester and his son, for the cop, for the hater, for the whole racist, trans-phobic, hetero-normative world.

WE LEFT OUR LOVE IN LOURMARIN

We left our love in Lourmarin wandering the castle walls,
walking slowly up the winding stairs, leaning out to touch
the gargoyle's nose. On Sunday mornings she likes to ring
the ancient church bells to beckon true believers.

Sometimes she stops for dessert on the outdoor patio
where every bite exploded on our tongues. Or she shops
for yogurt and pastries just beyond the town square
where I picked you up when you broke your knee.

On sunny afternoons she meanders the olive groves
and whistles a children's ditty about a half-collapsed bridge.
On cold nights she crouches in the corner of our former
        bedroom,
remembers us conjuring her until even tomorrow came.

Some days she drives up the hill to Bonnieux
just to see the view, then keeps going to the ghost town
of stone houses, imagining herself a Huguenot seeking
three tall cypresses—sign of shelter for the oppressed.

She's a little crazy, this one. Tends to repress the hard slog
of hospitals and flight delays and months of mending bones,
refuses to accept that something never mended right.
'It only looked perfect,' I try to tell her.

But she's not having it. 'It was,' she screams. 'It was.'
She vows to haunt me forever. 'Well, that's working,' I tell
        her.

'Can we just go get a latte?' she pleads.
'And some croissants with apricot jam?'

'All right already. I'll bring the car around to pick you up.
Don't forget your crutches. I'm tired of holding you up.'

DRIVING HOME ON HILLCREST

I see you washing dishes at your window
framed like a Hopper nighthawk

the sight of you as shocking as a sudden fall
or a harvest moon rising over a vacant field.

I've spent so much time thinking of you
I almost forgot you exist.

Is there another me inside of you?
Do you ever cook for her?

Do we eat on yellow plates?
Fight about the messes I make?

I want to fly to the farthest star,
but instead I race for home.

Tonight the moon is an iceball,
flung hard and headed my way.

AWAITING WORD AT MISSION CONTROL

I just saw 'Hidden Figures.' You'd love it,
I write in a text. You wanted to work for NASA
back when girls were steered toward other stars.
We went to the space center four years ago,
stood on the concrete pad below the platform
where Apollo astronauts blasted off for the moon.

Five, four, three, two, one . . .

Silence

as deep and dark as the back of the moon
or the lack of response from John Glenn
as he circled the Earth in Friendship 7.

Day 2: Heard you were having surgery
at Mayo. Maybe you didn't see my text.
Maybe your daughter deleted it.

Day 3: Millions of women are marching
all over the world. I share a link on Facebook
and up pops a *like* from your daughter's wife—
the first from the family in years.
I search her page for signs of life, find my ex-
granddaughter, almost four now.
She might as well live on Mars,
will never know I held her.

Day 4: A ding from Messenger! Not you.

Day 5: Another ding! This time it's my old friend
Susie, who watched the first moon landing
in my living room forty-eight years ago,
then left me stranded in adolescence,
set the coordinates for a lifetime
of losses. Never did learn why she left.
I would have killed for communication.

Day 6: *Roger, roger, come in, Amy.*
Are you running out of resentment yet?
Forty years from now I'll be ninety-nine.
What *is* the half-life of caring?

HE REMEMBERS; DOES SHE?

Someone posts a video of skating on Green Pond,
ice as smooth as the day we crossed that lake,
my brother and I, sixteen and going on eight.

And, oh, sweet Jesus, he remembers:
Mom dropped my sister and me off at the lake
after school so we could skate from the village
to the point between the coves and back.

That December evening—sunset blazing,
ice cracks booming, my fuzzy mitten tucked
inside his leather glove—was utter joy.
Till the day he stopped speaking to me.

What good is a memory tainted by pain?

The day my wife left I stared at the sun-beaten snow,
saw a storehouse of memories melting away.
Tried to tell myself it was my life too,
that our past wouldn't dissolve with our future.

But where would it live?
And who'd want to hear the stories?

My brother and I are friends again,
and today, at last, I heard him say it:
The best skating experience of my life.

Mine too, Pete.
I remember holding your hand
and flying across the ice.

DEAR AMY,

Remember that yard art Elizabeth gave us
for our wedding? I still put it in the garden
every spring. The hula girls have fallen off
and the handmade base broke in two
a few years ago. I found a new one,
but it's not as beautiful or strong
and it leaves the canoe looking tippy.
One of the angels has flown off,
the other's dangling by a thread.
But the silver bells are settled
in the boat, and the beaded heart
never fades, even in the rain.

LOSING THE SUGAR MAPLE

I stopped weeding the garden after you left,
though I tried to save the sugar maple,
even when its trunk had split nearly to the ground.

I'd never known such abundant shelter.
Adored that maple's graceful branches, its fiery
autumn leaves. Knew the hostas would brown
and wither without its summer shade.

But when that tree dropped a branch on the kitchen roof,
I knew it was time. Felt the thunder from the basement.
The day the tree guys came I could hardly watch.

Kept thinking of the squirrel that lived near the top.
Next time I saw him his tail was short and spindly.
He rarely runs the back fence anymore,
and I can barely walk a block.

It's a scary world—chainsaws, old age, arthritis.
I planted a Kwanza cherry near the chewed-up
stump. I'm hoping it blossoms next spring.

In the meantime I've wrapped the trunk
in crinkly paper to shield it from scald.
It's dangerous to stop being dormant—
that's when the sun can kill.

HOLDING PATTERN

Four years I've clung to this house as if it were you,
as if I could hold you by loading dishes the way you did,
keeping the walls the same colors.

I still have the first set of keys you made me.
The tag has a heart and your handwriting on it:
The keys to our kingdom.

On Facebook you're showing off a new key.
Wearing clothes I've never seen.

I want to crawl inside that photo,
lay my head on your new shirt.

Forty-eight years I lived without you
before the day we met. You'd think
it would have prepared me.

But, no, I'm like that fawn we saw
standing stock-still by the river.

Is it real? you asked.
It was. We were just floating by.

APRIL COMES AGAIN TO HOGSETT LAKE

and turtles are out by the hundreds
warming their blood in afternoon sun:
spiny softshells, red-eared sliders,
painted ones with brush strokes
of yellow on necks and legs.

As I guide my kayak past the shore,
they slip from muddy beds,
plop from weathered logs
and broken docks, then pop
their heads to inspect my boat.

Some I spot beneath the surface
swimming slowly beside me.
Others race to escape
my shadow, disappearing
into weeds and muck.

The turtles are as big as pie plates,
as small as teacups, some shells
etched by propeller blades.
One guy lets me get so close
I'm sure he must be dead.

And then I see him blink.
He stares at me but never leaves
his perch as I peruse his shell,
his gnarled limbs, his courage.
I wonder where he learned it.

I prefer the camouflage of weeds,
the shelter of mud, wish I knew
how to relax in the sun,
which kind of paddler to trust,
how to outrace the shadows.

REMNANTS OF A DREAM
OVERTAKE THE DAY

and just like that a veil is lifted and there you are—as real
as Paris or Jersey traffic or the cabin at Ford Lake with daisies
on the table and our dog asleep on the couch, his legs chasing
yesterday's rabbits. In my dream last night you ran from me
along a shoreline, your blue jacket a blur against red
snow-fence slats, the long hair you never had flying out
behind you—a silver flag I couldn't catch. Then you
turned and it was autumn, Lake Michigan was liquid,
and you tripped in the swash in an apricot coat
and when I reached for your hand, you let me.

UNDERPAINTINGS

Since you left I've filled the empty spaces in the house—
hung a landscape where your photo took us up the steps to
        Sacré-Cœur.
hid the pictures of our summer trip behind a naked lady done
        in oil,
bought a china cabinet to fill the place where you once played
        piano.

I plan to line the shelves with my mother's teacups, vases,
        plates.
Remember that day I took you to her childhood farmhouse in
        New Jersey?
How she told us later we'd seen the room where she was born?
I didn't know it till our trip was over.

*

I've taken a painting class to fill my time.
Just finished a piece showing the place where we ate breakfast
every morning in Provence. It's missing the strawberries
and giant blue cups, the croissants with apricot jam.

It's meant to signal transformation, its black-tinged tunnel
leading to a sunny courtyard the color of Van Gogh
        wheatfields,
its blue door the hue of fabric we bought in Avignon
or some other town. I can't remember. I relied on you for that.

*

Do you still wear your black-and-white raincoat?
I know we bought that in Bonnieux. I can picture the store
on a hill by a bend in the road. The jacket matched your hair.
We celebrated with a Niçoise salad and valley of tiled roofs.

That tunnel painting was supposed to be about my life after
        you—
the damp darkness of those first few years, the longed-for
        light,
a door to another world. But you're always that courtyard,
always that sunlight, always those wheatfield walls.

Epilogue

FUNERAL DIRECTIVE FROM A SERIAL MONOGAMIST WHO NEVER STOPPED LOOKING FOR THE ONE WHO WOULD LAST

Come sit in the front row, darlings.
I hope you all can fit. Bring your boxed-up
photos, useless house keys, sad CDs.
Lay your offerings at my feet.

Place your grievances on pure white
paper, fold them into mourning doves
or cut them into snowflakes and let
a blizzard fly. I'll keep still this time.

Pile a column of rocks in the corner
like that one we found in Algonquin.
Let it hold every sorrow, every regret
from this raggedy life.

Build a bulletin board of birch bark
from Fisherman's Island. Find a photo
of the oak tree at Sleeping Bear Dunes
where you lost an earring in the sand.

Show the orange trees at Phoenix Airport,
the sandhill cranes at Baker Lake,
a West Virginia mountain cabin
with my mother's pork chops in the oven,

that Sunday morning shower after church
when I shed my red silk dress—
well, maybe keep that one to yourself.
You know who you are.

Pick a preacher who's heard of Meg Christian
or at least the Dixie Chicks. Choose scripture
on forgiveness, hymns of consolation.
Make grace seem irresistible.

At the end of the service take off my glasses
and lay them on the casket. Pretend
it's a nightstand. Sing me to sleep.

ACKNOWLEDGMENTS

Thank you to the editors of the following publications in which these poems first appeared:

Midnight Circus: "Those first seven months"
Shut Down Strangers & Hot Rod Angels: An Anthology Inspired By the Songs of Bruce Springsteen (Bone & Ink Press): "Driving to the Jersey Shore"
Melancholy Hyperbole: "We could have burned the house down," "Gone," and "Uncoupling"
The Poeming Pigeon: "Two days after a canceled knee replacement"
The 3288 Review: "At the top of Sleeping Bear Dunes"
Amsterdam Quarterly: "Dateline Kalamazoo"
Blue Heron Review: "If *friend* had as many variations as Arctic snow"
New Verse News: "After the Confederate flag came down"
The Moon Magazine: "Funeral directive from a serial monogamist who never stopped looking for the one who would last"

✳

Portions of "Singing back to the 'straight' girl" were published in *Scarlet Literary Magazine,* as part of an earlier poem titled "Singing back to the siren."

"Shooting angels: Mendon, Michigan" appeared in "A Sense of Place: Poetry-Inspired Art," an exhibit at the Portage (Michigan) District Library.

"Wonderland" was first published in my chapbook *Fly Me to Heaven By Way of New Jersey* (Celery City Books), under the title "Susie and me in Wonderland."

"The alchemists had nothing on you" was printed in a broadside series that was part of an artist and writers' initiative called Alchemy. The broadside was exhibited at Western Michigan University's Richmond Center for the Arts, in Kalamazoo, and at the Box Factory for the Arts, in St. Joseph, Michigan.

"Carrying home to Hogsett Lake" appeared in a broadside series that was part of an artists and writers' initiative called Home. It was exhibited at the Richmond Center for the Arts, the WMU Homer Stryker School of Medicine, and the Carnegie Center for the Arts (Three Rivers, Michigan).

"Underpaintings" appeared in the book *Alchemy*, published by the Alchemy initiative.

*

Thank you to Diane Seuss for igniting my poetry writing with her smart and inspiring workshops and to John Rybicki for feeding the flame. Many thanks also to the women of my writing group, Poetry Dawgs, for their enduring support and astute critiques. I'm particularly grateful to Susan Ramsey and Jennifer Clark for reviewing the manuscript for this book and helping me make it sing.

ABOUT THE AUTHOR

Margaret DeRitter is the poetry editor and copy editor of *Encore,* a regional magazine based in Kalamazoo, Michigan. She was a winner of the 2018 Celery City Chapbook Contest, sponsored by Kalamazoo's Friends of Poetry, for her chapbook *Fly Me to Heaven By Way of New Jersey.* Her writing has appeared in the anthologies *Surprised By Joy* (Wising Up Press) and *Queer Around the World* (Qommunicate Publishing) and in a number of journals, including *The 3288 Review,* which nominated her poem "At the top of Sleeping Bear Dunes" for a Pushcart Prize. DeRitter has also written numerous magazine and newspaper articles. She worked for 22 years at the Kalamazoo Gazette and has taught journalism at Western Michigan University and Kalamazoo College. She was born and raised in New Jersey and has lived in Michigan since college. When not writing or editing, she often paddles Michigan lakes and rivers.

ABOUT THE PRESS

Unsolicited Press is a small press in Portland, Oregon that publishes exemplary fiction, poetry and creative nonfiction.

Learn more at www.unsolicitedpress.com.

CPSIA information can be obtained
at www.ICGtesting.com
Printed in the USA
LVHW091825120320
649865LV00005B/1007